# Digital Marketing Explained

## A Comprehensive Guide to Digital Marketing for Beginners

### Koso Brown

Copyright 2024© Koso Brown

All rights reserved. This book is copyrighted and no part of it may be reproduced, distributed, or transmitted in any form or by any means, including photocopying, recording, or other electronic or mechanical methods, without the prior written permission of the publisher, except in the case of brief quotations embodied in critical reviews and certain other non-commercial uses permitted by copyright law.

**Printed in the United States of America Copyright 2024© Koso Brown**

# Contents

Introduction .................................................................... 1
Chapter 1 ....................................................................... 3
Significant Events ........................................................ 3
    Definition of Digital Marketing .............................. 5
Chapter 2 ....................................................................... 9
Planning, Implementing, and Optimizing Your Digital Marketing Program .................................................... 9
    How Do You Approach Digital Marketing? ........... 11
Chapter 3 ..................................................................... 18
Key Distinctions Between SEM and SEO ................. 18
    What do SEM and SEO mean? ............................. 18
Chapter 4 ..................................................................... 22
SEO and SEM Tasks and Responsibilities ............... 22
Chapter 5 ..................................................................... 24
How a Small Business Can Gain from Digital Marketing .......... 24
    Why is digital marketing important so much to small businesses? ............................................................. 25
Chapter 6 ..................................................................... 29
What Impact Is Digital Marketing Having on Consumer Behavior? ................................................................... 29
    Problems that Digital Marketing Can Solve ......... 34
Conclusion .................................................................. 38

# Introduction

Digital marketing is becoming a crucial component of today's business and marketing strategy for connecting and interacting with consumers across the globe. Online platforms are now at the forefront of marketing strategies due to the revolutionary changes brought about by the digital age in the way businesses promote their goods and services. But have you ever pondered when year this incredible voyage started? Digital marketing is an all-encompassing approach that connects with target audiences and promotes goods and services through a variety of online platforms. Businesses and brands use digital channels, such as websites, social media, search engines, email, and mobile apps, to engage and interact with potential customers in today's technologically advanced world. Through efficient marketing strategies including search engine optimization (SEO), content marketing, social media marketing, email marketing, and pay-per-click (PPC) advertising, the objective is to raise brand awareness, improve website traffic, and boost conversions. Marketers may assess the success of their campaigns and make data-driven decisions for ongoing development with the help of data analytics. One effective and dynamic way to survive in the constantly changing digital landscape is through online marketing. We embark on an engrossing journey through the evolution of marketing in the digital age as we unravel the history of digital marketing. Everything started in the 1990s with the development of websites and the Internet. Search engines appeared as technology developed, opening the door for search engine optimization (SEO) tactics. Social media platforms emerged in the early 2000s, altering communication and bringing social media marketing into the picture. Mobile marketing gained traction as mobile devices became more widely used. The development of online marketing has been marked by several significant turning points and developments that have shaped the field's current state of flux and complexity as both consumer behavior and technological advancements continue to evolve.

# Chapter 1

# Significant Events

The idea of sending promotional messages electronically first emerged in the early days of computing, which is when online marketing first emerged. But the internet's advent in the 1990s was what set the foundation for the current state of online marketing. An important turning point was the 1994 introduction of the first clickable banner ad, which completely changed online advertising. Email marketing became popular as a result, offering a direct channel of contact for prospective clients.

Search engine optimization, or SEO, became necessary to raise website ranks as a result of the dominance of search engines like Google and Yahoo as technology advanced. A new era of social media marketing was brought about by the emergence of social media platforms in the early 2000s, which revolutionized the way brands engaged with their target customers.

Mobile marketing was made possible by the mobile revolution and involves tailoring advertisements to smartphone users. The development of data analytics gave marketers the ability to track and evaluate the effectiveness of their campaigns, enabling data-driven decision-making.

Hyper-personalization and automation are made possible by the combination of artificial intelligence (AI) and machine learning, which is still driving advancements in digital marketing today. The development of Internet marketing has been an ongoing process, and significant turning points have influenced how companies interact with their customers in the digital era.

Digital marketing's history is an amazing story of creativity and adaptation. Online marketing has evolved significantly to satisfy the ever-changing needs of the digital age, starting from its early beginnings with the introduction of electronic messaging and continuing through revolutionary turning points like the creation of the first clickable banner ad. Using technology like data analytics, social media, and mobile marketing has revolutionized how firms interact with consumers and develop memorable campaigns. In today's marketing environment, digital marketing is a potent and dynamic force that increases brand recognition, website traffic, and conversions. Online marketing has even more potential in the future as technology develops, to provide more individualized and targeted experiences for companies and their clients in the ever-expanding digital realm.

## Definition of Digital Marketing

Reaching out to customers using electronic media and the internet is known as digital marketing. These days, social media, online apps, email, search engines, and mobile applications are all inexpensive ways to advertise your company and interact with clients. In the modern business world, having a deeper understanding of digital marketing is beneficial.

In terms of how digital marketing functions, it is determined by the goal that your marketing team wishes to accomplish. Marketers advertise their goods and services through a variety of digital platforms. A marketing strategy is created to do this after the cross-channel digital landscape is examined. To gain insight into how to carry out the digital marketing plan, the behavior of the target audience is closely scrutinized.

Several digital marketing strategies are used to contact them and advertise the goods and services when the insight is obtained. Search Engine Optimization (SEO), Search Engine Marketing (SEM), Pay-per-click (PPC), Social Media Marketing (SMM), Affiliate Marketing, Email Marketing, and so on are a few of the often-utilized digital marketing strategies. Each of these has been covered in further detail in the sections that follow.

With the aid of these strategies, digital marketers can provide the sales team with high-quality leads. Measuring the effectiveness of marketing initiatives is a crucial component of how digital marketing operates. Digital marketers track and evaluate the effectiveness of social media efforts using technologies like Google Analytics. The entire process of digital marketing operates in this manner.

**Digital Marketing Types and Components**

Digital marketing comes in various forms. If you are a vendor, mastering these strategies will undoubtedly provide you with a competitive advantage and advance your knowledge of digital marketing. Additionally, it will help you understand how digital marketing functions. Let's briefly review some of the methods that educate you on how to use digital marketing.

**Email marketing:** The target customer receives a variety of emails. It can be an email sent to greet new clients, an instructive email with information about sales and discounts, or a letter of subscription used for blocks.

**Affiliate marketing:** This involves profitably promoting another person's goods or services on your channel or website.

**Pay-per-click (PPC) advertising:** PPC refers to sponsored advertisements that appear in search engine results. Publishers receive payment each time a user clicks on one of their ads.

**Social media marketing (SMM):** is the process of promoting our brand on social media sites. Using this social media platform, influencers with a large following can also work in sponsored partnerships to promote specific goods and services.

**Content Marketing:** We release our products through blogs, eBooks, infographics, and other channels. Increasing traffic growth and raising product awareness are two ways that content marketing aims to boost the client base through lead creation. To have an advantage in the market, a solid content marketing plan is essential.

**Search Engine Marketing (SEM):** SEM is the practice of placing adverts on search engine results pages (SERPs), or result pages of search engines. For this, a tiny margin must be paid. This is a sponsored campaign in which our product is advertised to the appropriate consumers who use their search engine terms to inquire about comparable products. There are numerous distinctions between SEM and SEO.

**Search Engine Optimization (SEO):** SEO is the process of getting your website ranked higher in search results, drawing more visitors because it shows up first in the search results, thereby increasing website visibility. Websites, infographics, and blogs can all be used for the same purpose.

# Chapter 2

## Planning, Implementing, and Optimizing Your Digital Marketing Program

**Planning**

Planning is essentially outlining or sculpting the digital marketing campaign. It entails taking into account the following things:

- During the planning stage, the digital marketing program's complete schedule and roadmap are laid out.
- Digital marketers make decisions on the allocation of funds and marketing expenditures in collaboration with other stakeholders.
- Determining what is actionable is another aspect of planning.
- In what way will the program for digital marketing be designed and organized? This is also decided upon throughout the planning stage.
- Planning the digital marketing channels to advertise the goods and interact with customers is the next and most important step. This gives digital marketers a better chance to accomplish their objectives quickly.

- When organizing a digital marketing campaign, developing a digital strategy is crucial.
- Digital marketers must plan with a wider scope of company objectives in mind. The three stages of these objectives are short-, medium-, and long-term.

**Implementing**

The execution phase begins after the planning is complete and the digital marketing program has been given a suitable structure. It is essential to apply the appropriate strategies at the appropriate times. Here, the following things should be taken into account:

- Lead nurturing and generation are crucial components of the implementation stage. The foundation of all marketing capabilities is made up of these two.
- Email marketing is one of these strategies that is automated throughout the execution stage.
- Advertising, email marketing, content marketing, web analytics, etc. are all started with caution.
- There are several marketing campaigns, SEO campaigns, social media campaigns, and so forth.
- Using a variety of channels, digital marketers launch

marketing and promotion during the implementation phase to achieve the objectives set forth during the planning phase.

## Optimization

It takes more than just creating and implementing a digital marketing plan to achieve long-term success. Monitoring and tracking the results of your digital marketing campaigns is crucial. To determine whether you have established the proper goals, it is also crucial to carefully analyze the performance and outcomes of your digital marketing strategies. If the outcomes fall short of expectations, digital marketers have the option to go back and review the plan to address any issues. This promotes the best possible use of financial and human resources.

## How Do You Approach Digital Marketing?

Now that you've learned, it's time to put your newfound knowledge to use and launch your firm. Let's tackle the topic of how to start digital marketing step by step. If you are a seller or can picture yourself as an entrepreneur, continue reading to have a better knowledge of the next steps in digital marketing.

**Establish your Objective**

It is critical to identify the objective of your digital marketing effort. Is your goal to rank #1 on Google searches, gain more likes, followers, or email responses, or are you just interested in building your brand and generating leads? Prioritize brand awareness above all else. The success of your brand awareness approach will be demonstrated when consumers substitute your brand name for the generic term. A prime illustration of this is what Google has accomplished. These days, instead of saying "Search it," people say "Google it." Although achieving this level of awareness takes time, it is possible.

How persuading takes place is through advertising. Lead generation is a crucial phase in the conversion process. It raises consumer awareness of your brand, educates them about your goods, and ultimately persuades them to buy it.

Thus, before moving on to other phases of digital marketing, it is imperative to have a defined objective.

**Describe the Audience You Hope to Reach**

You need to be mindful of who your target clientele is. Doing a consumer analysis is crucial. This can be achieved by researching the target market of your competitors and using tools such as Google Analytics and SEMrush to analyze the traffic to your website.

In the end, you need to choose at this stage of your digital marketing plan whether to target audiences or other businesses. Make sure your company has a clear, defined target market.

Developing a buyer character from the target audience research is also crucial. This includes defining the buyer's age, demographics, interests and dislikes in their line of work, employment and economic level, aspirations, and digital activity, among other things. To achieve flawless outcomes, this lengthy stage calls for patience and practice

**Define your Budget**

Campaigns involving digital marketing require an appropriate budget to be established. If you intend to work with a digital marketing business, that will be an expense. You will also have to pay to run the Google or Facebook ads.

For this reason, it's critical to allocate a reasonable sum to digital marketing initiatives. Before you spend any money on your digital marketing plan, take into account other elements such as trends, historical data, and statistics.

**Identify your marketing channel.**
It is important to carefully consider your target demographic when choosing the specific channel, you wish to use for your digital marketing strategy. Utilizing as many channels as you can is preferable.

Differentiating the channels, you utilize for business-to-business and business-to-consumer transactions is crucial. Blending all the available channels with a small focus on the media that your target audience uses most frequently would be the best approach to selecting the best channel for your business.
You may create a powerful strategy that increases your return on investment by properly integrating all the channels.

**Do research on keywords PPC and SEO**
When Google or other search engine adverts are displayed, this becomes important. Researching the keywords that your target audience uses to look for also improves search engine optimization.
You can learn more about the most common questions

regarding a given issue by visiting websites such as Answer the Public.

Reaching the top spot in the search results can be facilitated by having a thorough awareness of the objectives of your target audience as well as the specific terms they use to find you.

After the keywords are compiled, the monthly search volume and keyword difficulty must be compared. A better ranking for any keyword with a high monthly search volume and little competition can be obtained.

On the other hand, with pay-per-click, the goal is to reach as many people as possible while also lowering the cost per click.

After that, you need to optimize your website and fix other problems with it, like slow page loads and poor usability on mobile devices. Many software programs are available for use. Google is now providing free additional brand value assistance for our product.

You would get the desired outcomes if you relied on search engine optimization specialists.

**Create advertising or content for social media.**

It's time to start making ads for your digital marketing strategy that will interact with and sway your target audience. Selecting lookalike clients is crucial when starting small and gradually growing your clientele.

You can also rely on influencers in this situation, but before pursuing sponsored promotions, a thorough investigation of the influencer is required. Content quality should never be compromised, since this is one of the worst blunders to avoid. The clarity and ease of comprehension of a language or communication medium is a sign of quality. It is very forbidden to produce promos and ads just to increase the quantity of advertising. Videos, blogs, infographics, and images can all be used as ads. Make sure to include some fun, creative, and high-quality content to liven it up.

**Manage and keep an eye on your social media accounts.** Maintaining your brand's reputation is crucial. It can be developed by the regularity of your social media interactions and postings. It's critical to acknowledge both positive and negative reviews. "Your most dissatisfied customers are your greatest source of learning," as Bill Gates once stated.

Thus, it's critical to establish a relationship, solicit feedback from current clients regularly, and draw in new prospects at the same time. Other things to consider are the regularity of updates and adverts. Updates on the newest fashions and merchandise consistently bring in new clients.

**Don't overlook email advertising**

Email tracking is important for email marketing strategies. For instance, if someone visits your website to inquire about a specific product, you can send him emails with more information about sales or discounts.

Additionally, you can use email to persuade a customer to buy your product if they add it to their cart but then decide not to. Automated emails can further the goal and save time. Maintaining a presence in your clients' minds requires email marketing.

# Chapter 3

## Key Distinctions Between SEM and SEO

Businesses may utilize SEO and SEM, two other marketing channels that are occasionally used interchangeably, to connect with their target audience on search engines like Google and Bing.

## What do SEM and SEO mean?

Although SEO and SEM are two sides of the same coin, they are connected to different aspects of marketing and call for a significant amount of change.

The two titles are occasionally used synonymously to refer to the same set of activities, which is confusing to those of us who are new to the world.

What are the differences between Search Engine Marketing (SEM) and Search Engine Optimization (SEO) then? How do the two communicate and work together?

Thus, let's investigate SEO vs. SEM and learn more about it in this reading.

## Search Engine Optimization (SEO)

An approach to ranking in search results that emphasizes natural processes. Regardless of the area of digital marketing you specialize in, SEO is a crucial part of any plan, and you should have some understanding of it.

Search Engine Optimization (SEO) is the process by which search engines "scan" content to ascertain how effective it is at drawing users. They rank websites based on a variety of factors, including keywords, tags, and link names, as well as how well they can generate organic traffic.

**Search Engine Marketing (SEM)**

Using this digital marketing strategy, a website can pay to appear in search results and increase its visibility on search engine results pages (SERPs).

Search engine marketing is a cost-effective strategy for a business to use its marketing budget because advertisers only pay for appearances that lead to visitors. Additionally, every visitor raises the website's ranks in organic search results. Customers who submit search queries aiming to find commercial information are in the greatest possible frame of mind to make a purchase, in contrast to other sites like social media where users are not specifically seeking something.

**The distinction between SEM and SEO**

When we discuss the distinctions between SEO and SEM, we are only discussing different forms of advertising.

Although SEM and SEO are often used interchangeably, SEM and SEO are different since SEM is solely concerned with paid advertising. While SEO focuses on gathering, monitoring, and evaluating organic (unpaid) traffic patterns, SEM is more focused on driving traffic through sponsored adverts.

Speed is one of the main distinctions between SEM and SEO.

It's a fact that SEO requires patience. It takes longer to complete. particularly if your website is new and has few backlinks.

A study found that it typically takes two years to get on Google's first page. Numerous pages with high rankings were initially released three years or more ago.

This does not suggest that getting a Google ranking will take two years. It should not take long to see results if you target relevant keywords and adhere to SEO best practices.

You might notice results from an active SEM (paid) campaign in a matter of clicks. If your bids are significant and they are authorized, your advertisement will show up in the search results quite quickly.

However, unless there is no competition, which is rare, SEO may take some time. The time it takes to get organic results after starting an SEO effort could be months.

SEO cannot be examined in the same way due to the nature of the algorithm. Testing is still crucial to an effective SEO strategy, of course, but it can't do the same things that PPC can.

# Chapter 4

## SEO and SEM Tasks and Responsibilities

maximizing return on investment (ROI) in sponsored search advertising by conducting experiments, collecting and evaluating data, and identifying trends and insights. Pay-per-click (PPC) campaigns and activities, as well as tracking, reporting, and analysis of website analytics.

The complete SEO strategy of the business is developed, implemented, and managed by search engine marketing specialists (SEO/SEM). They usually oversee a variety of responsibilities, including planning content marketing strategies, digital marketing, web analytics, link development, and keyword research.

**Best Practices for SEO and SEM**

- ❖ UX may directly help with SEO since Google detects when consumers begin "Pogo sticking" after coming to your website from the search results.
- ❖ Improving the user experience (UX) on your website can benefit SEO in two ways.
- ❖ Comparable to a real-time dashboard, the Search Console displays your website's performance in the

SERPs (Search Engine Results Pages).
- ❖ Avoiding repetitive info is one of the most important SEO best practices to keep in mind. If you are not using Google Search Console, you are doing SEO blindly.
- ❖ The set of tasks known as SEO best practices is intended to help raise a website's search engine rankings. Common search engine optimization best practices include on-site optimization, keyword research, and building backlinks to a website.
- ❖ Any SEM expert will tell you that keywords, ad copy, and optimizing for less expensive keywords and ad groups take up the majority of their labor. The goal of each of these actions is to get clicks.
- ❖ It's not surprising that the networks that sell ad space frequently influence digital marketing techniques, and getting as many clicks as possible is the main objective for marketers.
- ❖ To have a successful SEM campaign, you must first adopt a conversion technique.

# Chapter 5

**How a Small Business Can Gain from Digital Marketing**
The majority of businesses use the Internet to further their marketing plans. Using your online platform to reach more people than offline marketing is the best approach to getting recognized, whether you're offering a good or service or having an informational website.

Even if conventional marketing techniques like print, radio, and TV can still be successful, there is an increasing awareness of the advantages that digital marketing can provide small firms.

**If you are a Small business owner hoping to grow, what can you do?**

Regardless of the size of your company, using digital marketing tools like social media, Pay Per Click (PPC), and Conversion Rate Optimization (CRO) is a terrific approach to update your marketing strategy and reach new consumers. Although some companies may believe that digital marketing is just for large companies with even larger resources, digital marketing may also be an effective tool for smaller companies. Digital marketing can help level the playing field and assist businesses with smaller budgets in reaching a larger audience.

To understand why digital marketing is so beneficial for small businesses, have a look at our list of the top outcomes that your firm may attain by implementing digital marketing methods.

## Why is digital marketing important so much to small businesses?

**Increased ROI (return on investment)**

One further alluring benefit of employing digital marketing tactics for small enterprises is the ability to increase brand awareness at a reduced expense.

Expense-intensive advertising campaigns are no longer required for small firms looking to make a rapid impression. Instead, your chances of success in sales are much higher if you use digital marketing to target your ideal client.

It is more important than ever to master the fundamentals of digital marketing to improve brand recognition, as many services in this field are either free or extremely inexpensive. The difference might be enormous when it comes to budgeting and having complete control over the use and timing of digital marketing tactics. On the other hand, managing your digital marketing through a specialized firm like One2create might also be more affordable. You can then access a multitude of information as a result, saving you the time and trouble of doing it yourself.

Knowing your target and figuring out the best approach to market to them is the most crucial component of digital marketing, and both large and small firms can do this as long as they have the necessary resources.

This implies that you can use online marketing to guarantee a higher return on investment by taking the time to get to know your customer base. According to Ann Smarty, a well-known figure in the field of digital marketing, "the great thing about digital marketing is that ingenuity and creativity can always win over big marketing budgets," in an essay she published for the Digital Marketer.

**Flexible and Adaptable**

Conventional marketing techniques are still quite effective at reaching new audiences, but once they are out there, they can be expensive, time-consuming, and often hard to edit or modify.

It is extremely advantageous for small businesses to be able to modify their strategies in response to shifting market conditions and customer preferences.

Nothing is fixed in stone when it comes to digital marketing. You may easily rewrite and republish anything you need to do to get better outcomes with a few clicks. Furthermore, your approach may be adjusted in response to emerging trends or new product releases, which makes expanding your business and staying current with your sector much easier. This enables you to maintain your plans current and effective in light of contemporary consumer trends by utilizing the progress tracking we previously discussed. This is frequently easier to accomplish for smaller companies with more specialized clientele than for larger companies with a wider target market.

**Simple Tracking of Progress**

The fact that you can easily see the effects of your digital marketing efforts is one of the biggest advantages for small businesses. Expensive print and television advertisements are difficult to gauge in terms of their numerical effectiveness since there is a lack of reliable, objective data. On the other hand, digital marketing provides crucial data on advancements, which is highly beneficial and a necessary instrument for growing your company.

Page visits, social media activity, and other metrics allow you to see what you're doing well and, more significantly, what needs to be improved at any given time. This enables you to be proactive with your marketing approach in addition to being able to respond appropriately. Monitoring the effectiveness of your digital marketing strategy will enable you to spot opportunities for growth and take appropriate action when the time is right.

**Increased Visibility**

Reaching potential consumers is made easier with digital marketing, which is undoubtedly one of the main advantages for small businesses.

Regardless of your location or product offerings, digital marketing creates new client opportunities and expedites outcomes.

By increasing your exposure on major search engines through techniques like SEO and PPC, you can typically make it simpler for potential customers to find you when looking for relevant products or locations. To make sure that your company is providing the appropriate material and answers online, a crucial component of this involves determining your target audience and then creating a list of efficient keywords and queries.

# Chapter 6

## What Impact Is Digital Marketing Having on Consumer Behavior?

### Seek out impulsive marketing

Through community participation initiatives, customized messages, and individualized content, it also aids in the development of consumer relationships. Brands can engage with customers in real-time by using online platforms like blogs, websites, and social media channels like Facebook and Twitter to respond to questions and offer advice on how to use products. This facilitates the development of an emotional bond between the company and its clients.

Brands can effectively reach their desired target audiences with digital media marketing techniques like pay-per-click (PPC) advertising, which reaches target audiences quickly and easily regardless of geographic location, email campaigns tailored to specific customer segments, video content that tells engaging stories about products, and influencer marketing programs that utilize well-known figures from various communities.

### The Lack of Patience in Consumers

Research indicates that consumers value digital marketing's

convenience. Email, social media, and other internet channels are simple ways for businesses to connect with their customers. When given information on a product in an easily readable style, people are more likely to buy it. Businesses may also guarantee that content is relevant and engaging for each customer category by personalizing communications to target certain consumer groups.

Businesses can connect with their target customers through email campaigns or free social media posts that offer timely updates about their goods and services. As a result, chances for higher sales conversions are created that are not available through conventional marketing communication channels.

**Client Loyalty That Is Not Reliable**
Customers can now readily obtain information about a company and its products thanks to the Internet. When it comes to purchasing goods, this enables individuals to make more educated choices. People can decide whether a product is worth the money by reading online reviews. To expand their consumer base and raise their brand awareness, businesses can also employ e-marketing strategies like social media campaigns and online advertising.

In addition, consumers are increasingly more likely to rate and review the goods they buy. This is a result of merchants being more open about their partners, the materials that go into making a product, and how those goods will be handled in transit.

**The Overall Word-Of-Mouth**
Gaining the trust of your customers can be accomplished through social proof. User-generated content (UGC) such as product reviews, consumer testimonials, or referrals from friends and family can serve as social proof. The more brand testimonials you receive, the more positive perceptions you will have and the more trust you will gain from prospective clients.

Businesses may now interact with their customers in a more meaningful and individualized way thanks to digital marketing. Businesses can design highly targeted campaigns with information catered to particular interests or demographics. They can also monitor consumer behavior through a variety of channels, which enables them to modify their approach in light of the information they have gathered.

**Consumers Search for Comments and Reviews**

Strong web presences enable companies to interact with their audience more directly, which increases customer engagement. Businesses may collect real-time client feedback through a variety of platforms, including email newsletters and chatbots, which helps them make better decisions for upcoming product launches and marketing efforts.

All things considered, regardless of size or industry, having a strong internet presence is essential for any successful business today. To be competitive in the current market scenario, businesses must make sure they give accurate information about themselves and their products and interact with customers regularly to earn their trust and establish lasting relationships.

**Customers Are carrying out Internet Research**

Before making a purchase, consumers often look for reviews, ratings, and price comparisons. Because of this, companies must put a high priority on customer satisfaction to earn customers' faith in their goods and services. Businesses may build an online presence that will attract more customers and persuade them to choose them over rivals by offering reasonable rates, first-rate customer service, and ongoing industry updates.

**ROI of an Effective Digital Marketing Campaign**

Measuring the success of your digital marketing effort is crucial, as was covered in the sections above. There are some criteria you must consider to accurately determine the return on investment (ROI) of your digital marketing operation. Let's examine a few of these KPIs related to digital marketing:

- ❖ **Click-Through Rates:** A greater click-through rate (CTR) indicates that your piece or content is doing well and reaching a larger audience.
- ❖ **High Lead Closures:** The ultimate deal closure that occurs when the marketing team transfers leads to the sales team is referred to as a lead closure. A high lead rate indicates that the marketing team is closing most of the leads it passes along. This implies that the lead quality is high, which is a sign that the work you've put into your digital marketing is paying off.
- ❖ **Low Cost of Acquisition:** This indicates how much you spend on marketing each time a new client is acquired. A low cost of acquisition shows that the objectives of your digital marketing effort are being met.

❖ **High Return on Ad Spend (ROAS):** The total return on the amount of money spent just on advertising. A high ROAS indicates that your advertisements are effective and producing the desired outcomes.

## Problems that Digital Marketing Can Solve

Most of the issues that a business may face can be resolved by digital marketing. Its impact on issues that are vital to an organization's management is enormous. In this section, we will examine some of the primary issues that digital marketing may resolve:

### Having trouble producing high-quality content

There is a content-hungry audience. There won't be as much audience interaction with your material, though, if you are posting things at random without a clear content marketing plan in place. For this reason, digital marketing is crucial to producing relevant and captivating content for the intended audience.

**Unwanted outcomes of paid advertisements**

Even in situations where paid advertisements are ineffective, digital marketing can the capacity to increase visitors. Therefore, if you are spending money and receiving no traffic or returns, you must surely need it.

**Minimal Website Visits**

It's critical to drive the correct kind and volume of traffic to your website. If you do not use digital marketing, even with a beautiful and interesting website, you will not get any traffic. Low leads and thus low conversions are caused by lower traffic.

**Declining Conversion Rates**

Your sales staff is receiving low-quality leads, which translates into low conversion rates. The conversion rates will be low even with the best efforts of your sales team. Analytical tools are used in digital marketing to assist generate quality leads and improve conversion rates.

**Low social media account performance**

Customers are very engaged on social media because they are increasingly technically savvy. For this reason, having a strong social media presence is crucial for businesses. On the other hand, a poorly managed social media account may make it more difficult for you to establish a positive brand reputation with your target audience. Millions of start-ups worldwide have already benefited from social media marketing by maximizing their profitability. Therefore, if you are performing poorly on social media, your best option is to use digital marketing.

**Inability to maximize ROI**

Most businesses have already invested a significant amount of money in marketing, and they are headed toward daily spending increases without being able to optimize their profits. Digital marketing is necessary for these kinds of organizations. A thriving firm depends heavily on a high Return on Investment, and digital marketing offers the ideal strategies to get greater outcomes with less money spent.

## Conclusion

Gaining a basic understanding of the aforementioned strategies will help your company's marketing take off. A few numbers to round up this discussion: 15 million people worldwide presently use mobile phones, according to Statista.

You can therefore access the global market of 15 million clients by making a small investment in digital marketing. Therefore, never undervalue the importance of digital marketing in the corporate and marketing domains.

www.ingramcontent.com/pod-product-compliance
Lightning Source LLC
Chambersburg PA
CBHW050247230526
45470CB00005B/2155